I AM READING

Noisy Neighbours

NICOLA MOON

Illustrated by
LIZ MILLI

KINGFISHE

For Travis – N.M.
To Nana and Grandpa Sefton with all my love – L.M.

KINGFISHER
An imprint of Kingfisher Publications Plc
New Penderel House, 283-288 High Holborn
London WC1V 7HZ

This edition published by Kingfisher 2005
First published by Kingfisher 2003
2 4 6 8 10 9 7 5 3 1

A CIP catalogue record for this book
is available from the British Library.

ISBN 0 7534 1143 1

Printed in India
1TR/0505/AJANT/FR(SC)/115SM

Contents

Noisy Neighbours

George lived at Number Six,

Acorn Road.

He loved to sit in the garden and

do the competition in his magazine.

George dreamed that one day

he would answer all the questions

and win the big prize.

Louis lived next door to George. He loved to stand in the garden and play his trumpet. He dreamed that one day he would be a famous musician.

One day, George was sitting in the garden trying to do his competition, when . . .

TRAN-TARAAH!

George was so surprised that he dropped his pen in the daffodils.

"Oh, bother," he huffed.

TRAN-TRAN-TARAAH!

It was Louis, playing his trumpet.

"Excuse me, Louis," George called over the fence. "Please could you play more quietly? I'm trying to concentrate on my competition. It's very difficult today."

"Sorry," said Louis. "The trumpet isn't a quiet sort of instrument and I have to practise for a very important concert. Don't you think it's wonderful music?"

George didn't think it was at all wonderful.

"Humph!" he said, and went back to his competition.

TRAN-TRAN-TARAAH!

The music started up again, even louder than before.

"Humph! This is ridiculous!" George muttered, and he stomped indoors.

George made himself a pot of tea.

Then he opened a packet of

raspberry buns and settled down

in his armchair.

"At last I can concentrate!" he sighed.

9

The trumpet blared along
Acorn Road . . .

. . . and right into George's sitting-room.
"Oh no!" he groaned, covering his ears
with his paws.

Now he couldn't hear the trumpet –
but he couldn't hold his pen either.

Then he noticed the tea cosy.

"Perfect!" he said, pulling it over his ears.

The tea cosy made his head hot, but

at least it muffled the noise

TRUN-TRUN-TURUUH!

But not for long . . .

TRUN-TRUN-*VROOM-VROOM-WHIRR!*

"It's getting worse!" George moaned,

pulling off the tea cosy.

"How can I think with all this noise?"

He stomped to the bathroom and found

a big bag of cotton wool.

He was just stuffing some into his ears

when . . .

BANG-BANG-BANG!

Someone was at the door.

"What is it *now*?" George wailed.

It was Louis.

"Did you hear that dreadful noise?"

he asked. "How can a musician work

with *that* going on?"

"But . . ."

said George,

pulling cotton

wool out

of his ears.

"I thought it

was you."

"*Me*? You

think *I* . . ."

VROOM-VROOM-WHIRR!

A large, shiny motorbike came
roaring down Acorn Road.

It stopped outside Number Eight.

George and Louis stared.

Sitting on the bike was their
new neighbour.

"Hi! I'm Harriet," she called.

"Do you like my bike?"

"Humph!" said George.

"It's a bit noisy. I was trying
to concentrate on a very
difficult competition."

"And I was trying to practise
my trumpet for a very important
concert," said Louis.

"Oh dear!" said Harriet.

"Motorbikes, trumpets and
competitions don't really mix,
do they?"

She thought for a moment.

Then she said, "Come in and have

a cup of tea. I have an idea."

"I hope it's a quick idea," mumbled

Louis. "I have a lot of practising to do."

"I hope it's a quiet idea," muttered

George. "I have a lot of

questions to answer."

8

"It's a very *good* idea," said Harriet, as they sat round her kitchen table. "On Mondays and Thursdays we will all try to be quiet so that George can do his competition."

"That *is* a good idea," said George. "On Tuesdays and Fridays Louis can play his trumpet as much as he likes," continued Harriet.

"That's an even better idea!" said Louis.

18

"On Wednesdays and Saturdays it will be my turn," said Harriet.
"I will be able to ride my bike and work on the engine all day long."

"What about Sundays?" asked George.
"Whose turn will it be on Sundays?"

"On Sundays," said Harriet, "we will all meet here for tea and cakes."

"That's the best idea of all," said Louis, who loved to eat cake.
"The very best idea," agreed George, who loved to drink tea.
"Then it's agreed," said Harriet.
"I'll see you both tomorrow."

On the way home, George stopped.

"What day is it tomorrow?" he asked.

"Sunday," said Louis.

"So . . . that means today is Saturday?"
said George.

"Oh no!" cried Louis.

"Oh . . . humph!" moaned George.

"Oh yes!" called Harriet,
putting on her helmet.
"Today is Saturday!"

VROOM-VROOM-VROOM-WHIRR!

Just in Time

George couldn't believe his eyes when
he opened his magazine one morning.
"WIN A TRIP TO MONSTER FUN PARK,"
he read. "ENTER OUR COMPETITION NOW!"

George had always wanted to go to Monster Fun Park. He was so excited that he put three spoons of marmalade into his tea and forgot to eat his toast.

The competition had one hundred questions! George sharpened all his pencils, wrote a notice that said "DO NOT DISTURB" and pinned it to his door. Then he settled down to work.

The competition was very difficult.

George concentrated very hard.

He didn't hear Louis playing his trumpet

on Tuesday.

He didn't hear Harriet riding her
motorbike on Wednesday.

By Thursday, only the two most
difficult questions were left.
George thought that Louis and
Harriet would be able to help.

George went next door to see Louis.

Harriet was there, helping Louis choose

a shirt for his concert.

"Do you think I should wear the sparkly

one, or the flowery one?" asked Louis.

"I like the spotty one," said Harriet.

"Yes, wear the spotty one," said George. "Now can you help me answer *my* questions? I could win a trip to Monster Fun Park."

"Monster Fun Park?" said Louis. "Wowee!"

"What are the questions?" asked Harriet.

George showed them his competition.

"A loud musical instrument, beginning
with T?" said Louis. "It's a trumpet."

"Of course!" said George.

"Thanks, Louis."

"A noisy machine with two wheels, beginning with M?" said Harriet. "It must be a motorbike!"

"That's it! Well done, Harriet," cried George.

George carefully wrote down the answers.
As he folded the answer sheet he noticed
the date at the top.

"Oh no!" he wailed. "We're too late!
The answers have to reach the magazine
office by twelve o'clock today.
I should have posted this yesterday."

"We can take it ourselves," said Harriet.

"But it's miles away!" said George.

"There isn't time."

"There is if we go on my bike," said

Harriet. "You can both ride in the sidecar."

Louis complained about being in
the sidecar.

"My legs are squashed," he moaned.

George complained about wearing
a helmet.

"My ears are squashed," he groaned.

"Stop fussing, or we'll be late," said
Harriet. "Now, hold tight!"

They roared to
the end of Acorn Road.

"Which way now?" asked Harriet.

"Right!" said George.

"Left!" said Louis.

"Follow the signs to the town centre,"
said George.

"But not so fast round the corners!"
wailed Louis, who was looking
a bit green.

They raced over the crossroads,
and whizzed round a bend.

"Stop!" cried George,
as the envelope flew
out of his paw and into a prickly bush.
George had trouble getting the envelope
out of the bush.
He kept getting prickles in his nose.

BIG COMPETITION,
PUZZLE WORLD,
10 THE HIGH STREET,
OAK TOWN

"Hurry up!" said
Harriet. "We don't
have much time!"

They roared up to the magazine office.

It was two minutes to twelve.

"Are we too late?" asked George.

"Not if you run!" said Harriet.

George puffed up the stairs
and handed in his
competition.
He was just
in time!

PUZZLE
WORLD

"Thank goodness for that!" said Louis.

"Can we go home now? *Slowly*, please!"

Soon they were sitting in Harriet's
kitchen enjoying large slices of
chocolate cake.
Louis, who was feeling better,
had two pieces.

"When will you know if you've won?"
asked Harriet.
"Not until next week," George sighed.

The next few days seemed very long.
Louis couldn't concentrate on playing
his trumpet.

Harriet couldn't concentrate on fixing
her motorbike.

George couldn't concentrate on anything at all. He thought he would burst with waiting.

Then at last one morning, a fat, gold envelope dropped onto the doormat. His paws were shaking as he tore it open and read:

"CONGRATULATIONS! YOU HAVE WON FIRST PRIZE."

George rushed outside.

Louis was there, helping Harriet polish her bike.

"Harriet! Louis! I've won! I'm going to Monster Fun Park!" he shouted.

"Well done, George!" said Louis and Harriet. "We knew you could do it."

"You both helped me win," said George, "and you're coming with me — I've got three tickets!"

They had a wonderful day at
Monster Fun Park.
"Hold tight!" said Harriet,
as they went on the roller coaster
for one last ride.

"This time I'm going to keep my eyes open!" said Louis.

"So am I," said George.

"Here we go!"

WHEEEEE!

MONSTER FUN PARK

About the Author and Illustrator

Nicola Moon used to be a science teacher, but now she writes books full time. She says, "I feel sorry for George with those noisy neighbours. But they are such special friends, I don't think he would ever change them. Do you?" Nicola's other books for Kingfisher include the I Am Reading titles *Alligator Tales and Crocodile Cakes* and *JJ Rabbit and the Monster*.

Liz Million loves illustrating children's books, and she regularly visits schools and libraries to talk about her work. She says, "George reminds me of my grandpa. He enjoys doing crossword competitions. Sometimes he wakes my nana up at night when he's trying to think of the answer to a difficult question. Poor Nana!"

Tips for Beginner Readers

1. Think about the cover and the title of the book. What do you think it will be about? While you are reading, think about what might happen next and why.

2. As you read, ask yourself if what you're reading makes sense. If it doesn't, try rereading or look at the pictures for clues.

3. If there is a word that you do not know, look carefully at the letters, sounds, and word parts that you do know. Blend the sounds to read the word. Is this a word you know? Does it make sense in the sentence?

4. Think about the characters, where the story takes place, and the problems the characters in the story faced. What are the important ideas in the beginning, middle and end of the story?

5. Ask yourself questions like:
Did you like the story?
Why or why not?
How did the author make it fun to read?
How well did you understand it?

Maybe you can understand the story better if you read it again!